20/2/15

T

D0533514

LAT

Please renew or return items by the date
shown on your receipt

www.hertsdirect.org/libraries

Renewals and
enquiries: 0300 123 4049

Textphone for hearing   0300 123 4041
or speech impaired

Hertfordshire

520 187 04 8

THE FIRST WORLD WAR AT SEA
IN PHOTOGRAPHS

1914

PHIL CARRADICE

AMBERLEY

Acknowledgements

Many of the photographs come from the J. & C. McCutcheon Collection. Any others are from the author's own collection.

First published 2014

Amberley Publishing
The Hill, Stroud
Gloucestershire, GL5 4EP

www.amberley-books.com

Copyright © Phil Carradice, 2014

The right of Phil Carradice to be identified as the Author of this work has been asserted in accordance with the Copyrights, Designs and Patents Act 1988.

ISBN 978 1 4456 2233 0 (print)
ISBN 978 1 4456 2256 9 (ebook)

British Library Cataloguing in Publication Data.
A catalogue record for this book is available from the British Library.

Typesetting by Amberley Publishing.
Printed in the UK.

Contents

Background

The first dozen or so years of the twentieth century were dominated – in the press, in Parliament and in the minds of the general public – by the great Naval Race, an unofficial but nevertheless very real contest between Britain and Germany to see who could build the greatest number of battleships and thereby achieve dominance on the high seas.

The Naval Race was arguably one of the most important contributing factors in the outbreak of the First World War and had its roots in a visit to Britain made by the German Kaiser, Wilhelm II, at the end of the nineteenth century. He came in the summer of 1897 to help celebrate the Diamond Jubilee of his grandmother Queen Victoria.

Kaiser Wilhelm had succeeded his father as Emperor of Germany on 15 June 1888, the country having been formed by the amalgamation of various fragmented Germanic states less than twenty years before. Germany was the strongest and, under its new Kaiser, potentially the most aggressive power in central Europe. However, while its army might be a formidable fighting machine – as victory in the recent Franco-Prussian War demonstrated – what it lacked was an effective and efficient navy.

When, on 26 June 1897, as part of the Diamond Jubilee celebrations for Victoria, the Kaiser attended the enormous Review of the British fleet at Spithead – 168 British capital ships and support craft gathered together in the lee of the Isle of Wight – he was immediately angry and, in his eyes at least, humiliated by the poor showing of the German Fleet.

Invitations to attend the Review had been issued to over twenty foreign navies and most of them had duly sent ships to represent them. Thousands of spectators took to the water in small boats to view, first of all, the USS *Brooklyn* with her sparkling white hull and tall, thin funnels and then steam around the enormous bulk of the Russian *Rossiya*. Pride of place, naturally enough, went to the British ships, glistening in their Victorian livery of black hulls, white upperworks and yellow funnels. So vast was the array of warships that nobody could ever hope to see all the Royal Navy vessels moored in the Solent. It did not stop them trying.

In contrast, nobody gave even a second glance to the handful of German ships that had made the journey across the North Sea. Dwarfed and strangely out of place, they looked drab and dingy in their dull grey paintwork. Small wonder the Kaiser was furious.

Kaiser Wilhelm II was a strange man, the product of a dysfunctional family and embittered by an accident at birth that had left him with a withered left arm. Almost as a substitute or surrogate for his damaged limb the Kaiser embraced militarism and from the time of his accession to his later abdication he was rarely seen out of uniform.

He had come to Britain at least once each year, for Cowes Week, ever since he became the German Emperor but this Jubilee Review was different. Now, when he gazed out from the deck of the Royal Yacht, Wilhelm saw line after line of British battleships, cruisers and destroyers, stretching for thirty miles across and down the Solent. The array of British ships stretched as far as the eye could see. And the Kaiser was consumed by jealousy. Then and there he decided that he had to have such a fleet in Germany.

The Kaiser was lucky in that he found a supporter for his ambitions in the shape of Grand Admiral Alfred von Tirpitz who, just a few weeks after the Jubilee Review, was appointed Secretary of State for the German Navy. Quickly picking up what his master wanted, the Admiral's aim – the Tirpitz Plan, as it was eventually known – became to create such a powerful German Navy that its mere presence in and around the North Sea would force Britain to accede to any German plan or aim anywhere in the world.

Tirpitz was a master in the art of brinkmanship. Coming to blows with such a mighty opponent as the Royal Navy, he reasoned, was neither desirable nor necessarily the main objective of the new German Navy. No matter how many dreadnoughts Germany built, ultimately she could not hope to match the strength and power of Britain.

Yet the threat of a powerful German presence in the North Sea was implicit. A fleet action of any sort would be bound to damage Britain's prestige and cause harm to her stock of battleships and her manpower. It should, therefore, be something to be avoided at all costs. But in order to make this threat realistic Germany would require, it was estimated, a fleet two-thirds the size of Britain's.

Beginning with the first Navy Bill in 1898, Tirpitz – backed by the proffering of his resignation should he not get his way – managed to force a succession of Acts through the Reichstag, voting money to build more and more ships for the German High Seas Fleet. By the beginning of the twentieth century the great Naval Race had begun.

Since 1805 Britain had relied upon the supremacy of its battle fleet to protect its coast, its possessions and its mercantile marine. And now, faced by Germany's clear declaration of intent, the men at the Admiralty felt they had no choice but to respond. Admiral Jacky Fisher, First Sea Lord, was clear what was needed: 'Germany keeps her whole fleet concentrated within a few hours of England. We must therefore keep a fleet twice as powerful within a few hours of Germany.' It was a clear declaration of the two power standard, the aim being to maintain a British navy that was at least the size of the next two most powerful navies in the world combined, in this case Germany and the United States of America.

The battleship *Dreadnought* was launched in 1906. She was a revolutionary new vessel with ten 12-inch guns – most other battleships had just four – thick armour plating and a top speed of 21.6 knots. She immediately made every other capital ship in the world totally redundant and gave Britain a healthy lead in the Naval Race but it was not one that was destined to last long. The Kaiser and Tirpitz were adamant – if Britain had dreadnoughts, Germany must have them, too.

It placed a huge burden on the German economy but in 1908 and 1909 German dreadnought building actually outstripped Britain's by seven to four. The Kaiser was beside himself, delirious with joy. He was not in the least concerned that the building programme was the cause of steadily worsening relations between Germany and Britain. He disliked his Uncle Bertie, who had succeeded Victoria in 1901, and saw no reason why his vibrant new country should be denied its 'place in the sun.' Building a powerful navy was part of that plan – and if the existence of that navy just happened to upset Britain, then so be it.

In 1909, news was leaked to the British press that the government was planning to build just four new dreadnoughts over the next few years. It caused outrage, both in the pages of the national newspapers and in the minds of the public, who were clear that their preferred number of such ships was eight. Opinions ran high. Hundreds of men and women paraded in front of the Admiralty chanting, 'We want eight and we won't wait.'

Thoroughly alarmed by the strength of public opinion, the government reconsidered its position. With his tongue pressed firmly in his cheek, Winston Churchill, First Lord of the Admiralty, later said that the economists offered four dreadnoughts, the Admiralty wanted six – and so they compromised on eight.

Jacky Fisher left the Admiralty at the beginning of 1910 but the Naval Race continued unabated. In 1911 five new British dreadnoughts were on the stocks; by 1913 that figure had risen to seven. German dreadnought building, on the other hand, had finally begun to slow down.

Faced by the growing military threat of Russia, Chancellor Theobald Bethmann Holweg was clear that more money would now have to be spent on the army in order to keep Germany's western borders intact. There was, he felt, a real possibility of Germany becoming isolated and vulnerable and so he began attempting to limit the naval rivalry and to form, instead, an understanding with Britain.

Arguably, the slowing down had little to do with Germany's perceived isolation in Europe. The Kaiser still wanted his fleet but by 1914 the country had achieved the two thirds parity with the Royal Navy that Admiral Tirpitz had originally decreed. On the eve of war in the summer of 1914 Britain had twenty-nine dreadnoughts available for service; Germany had nineteen – as well as numerous pre-dreadnoughts which, on both sides, made up the Reserve Fleets.

Battlecruisers – a new weapon of war that owed much to the fertile brain of Jacky Fisher – were much more closely matched, Britain having nine to Germany's seven. As far as cruisers and other vessels were concerned, there Germany had a decided advantage.

It was not so much numbers, but in terms of design, the German vessels were far superior. Naval planners in Britain had become obsessed with building bigger and better dreadnoughts and had fallen into the trap of virtually ignoring the development of cruisers, which were the workhorses and the defenders of the trade routes across the Empire.

Consequently, when it came to combat in 1914, the old British armoured cruisers were invariably too slow, too poorly armoured and fitted with inadequate weapons. It was to cost the Royal Navy dearly in the months to come.

Kaiser Wilhelm II of Germany, the son of Kaiser Friedrich III and Queen Victoria's eldest daughter, the Princess Royal, also called Victoria. The Kaiser, seen here on a railway station in the early months of the First World War, surrounded by members of his staff, was first cousin to both George V and Marie of Romania, as well as second cousin to Czar Nicholas of Russia. A vain, opinionated man, as soon as he succeeded to the throne in 1888, he began to lead Germany on a course that would make her into a modern and powerful sovereign nation. The Kaiser's Germany was to be a country whose strength was based on industrial and military might – and to achieve this she needed a navy to rival that of Britain.

The great Naval Review at Spithead, 26 June 1897. In this artist's impression, the ships of the Royal Navy stretch away in solid lines, battleships, cruisers and dozens of smaller craft. In all there were 165 of them and that was just the tip of the iceberg. Hundreds more ships of war were on duty across the world. In this illustration, the vessels of foreign powers lie anchored to the left of the British fleet, dwarfed and totally over-shadowed by the power of the Royal Navy. It was an awesome spectacle that nobody who saw it ever forget – least of all Kaiser Wilhelm, who came to celebrate his grandmother's Diamond Jubilee and left with the burning desire to give Germany a fleet to rival Britain's.

The Kaiser returned to Germany with one aim, to build up his navy. In the person of Admiral Alfred von Tirpitz, he found the man he needed to take charge of developments. Almost forty years old, after a distinguished career in the Prussian and German navies, Tirpitz immediately understood what the Kaiser wanted. As State Secretary of the Imperial Navy Office he ruthlessly drove forward the building programmes for dreadnoughts, cruisers and other craft. The British might make fun of his long forked beard but nobody doubted the sincerity – or the danger – of his intentions.

HMS *Dreadnought* of 1906 was the most revolutionary warship since the *Warrior*, the world's first iron man of war. With her massive 12-inch guns – clearly visible in this photograph – the *Dreadnought* made every other warship in the world obsolete overnight and gave Britain a major lead in the great Naval Race. Germany was not long in following the British example and soon she, too, began to build dreadnoughts.

Opposite page: Faced by a determined and ruthless foe, Britain and the other European nations responded in the only way they knew how: by building battleships to match Germany's and by forming alliances that, they thought, would give them protection. This cartoon from the immediate pre-war period takes an amusing look at the Entente Cordiale that was formed between Britain and France and at the German response to the alliance.

SOLID.

GERMANY. "DONNERWETTER! IT'S ROCK. I THOUGHT IT WAS GOING TO BE PAPER."

The cruiser *Dresden* is shown here in the Kiel Canal in the days before war was declared.

The War at Sea, 1914

By the last days of July 1914 it was clear that war was coming. On 27 July, the German High Seas Fleet was unceremoniously recalled from its summer cruise around Norway and sent to its war bases. A day later, the three British fleets – which had been taking part in a review at Spithead and exercises in the Channel – were also ordered to their war stations with a general naval mobilisation taking place on 1 August.

The Royal Navy was about as ready as it ever could be for the coming conflict. And yet, despite its numerical superiority, there were problems. The Navy of 1914 was hidebound by tradition and by a dangerous conservatism that ridiculed or even dismissed new techniques and new equipment. As Winston Churchill, First Lord of the Admiralty, was to later write, the Royal Navy was shackled by its traditional routines and by the glory of its past record. In Churchill's words, it meant that 'at the outbreak of the conflict we had more captains of ships than captains of war'. Nevertheless, when, at midnight on 4 August the message 'Commence hostilities against Germany' was flashed to all British ships there was a mood of optimism in the air. At long last the conflict that had been looming for years had finally arrived.

As if to emphasise the point, early on the morning of 4 August, Admiral Sir John Jellicoe was installed as commander of the Grand Fleet. He took over from Sir George Callaghan who, Churchill and Battenberg at the Admiralty had decided, was too old and not sufficiently robust to command Britain's greatest weapon in the coming war. Jellicoe was unhappy about the way it was all done but he did not refuse the command.

From the beginning of the conflict, the Royal Navy imposed a 'distant' blockade on the German coast, something that would, it was hoped, eventually bring Germany to the peace table. The Grand Fleet in the north, and the increasingly important forces of the Dover Patrol in the south, were the implements of the blockade, something that was largely successful in bottling up the German dreadnoughts in their base at Wilhelmshaven.

There were, however, several German units at large in different parts of the world. These included Admiral von Spee and his East Asiatic Squadron as well as raiders like the *Emden*, *Karlsruhe* and *Königsberg* in the Indian Ocean, the West Indies and on the coast of Africa. And, of course, the silent but deadly German U-boats were more than capable of slipping, unnoticed, past the patrolling vessels of the Royal Navy.

August

On the very first day of the war the light cruiser *Gloucester* detected the powerful German battlecruiser *Goeben* and her consort, the cruiser *Breslau*, in the Mediterranean. Locating the German ships was made possible by the interception of wireless transmissions, the first time the Royal Navy ever made use of such technology in time of war.

Finding the *Goeben* was one thing, catching her was another matter. A secret alliance between Germany and Turkey meant that Admiral Souchon on the *Goeben* had already decided to run for Istanbul (Constantinople as it then was). Before he went he shelled the French ports of Bone and Philippeville and then headed east. Luck was with him. Early on 4 August he encountered the British battlecruisers *Indomitable* and *Indefatigable* but as war between Britain and Germany had not yet been declared the four ships passed each other with little more than hostile glares.

Despite being shadowed by the British squadron, Souchon coaled at Messina, then sailed east once more. In a confused series of manoeuvres, the two German ships managed to evade the British cruiser screen and slip through the Dardanelles into Constantinople. Admiral Troubridge, who commanded the cruisers and had broken off the chase, was later court martialed, but acquitted, for his part in the affair, which had led to more than a few red faces at the Admiralty.

With the alliance between Germany and Turkey still a closely guarded secret, rather than intern the vessels it was announced that Turkey had just bought the *Goeben* and *Breslau*. The deception fooled nobody, particularly as the German crews remained on board, albeit clad in Turkish head gear, and a few months later the two vessels led the Turkish fleet in a bombardment of the Black Sea ports of Odessa and Sebastopol.

The opening days of the conflict brought both success and disaster for the Royal Navy. On 5 August the destroyer *Lance* fired the Navy's first shots of the war when she and the *Landrail* intercepted the converted German mine layer *Königin Luise* off the Thames Estuary. Aided by the light cruiser *Amphion*, the weight of British gunnery soon sent the *Königin Luise* to the bottom. Forty-six of her crew were rescued, twenty-one of them by the *Amphion*.

At 6.45 the following morning – 6 August – the *Amphion* became the first Navy casualty of the war when she struck one of the mines so recently laid by the *Königin Luise*. Her back was broken and the forward gun crew wiped out. The explosion also killed a large number of men taking breakfast in the forward mess hall – nineteen of the German survivors among them. Sinking by the head, Captain Cecil Fox had no alternative but to order 'Abandon Ship'. Unfortunately, the *Amphion* still had way on and, turning in a wide, slow arc, she ran full tilt into a second mine. A huge explosion rent the air and by 7.00 a.m. she had totally disappeared into the vastness of the North Sea.

On 7 August in the West Indies, the cruiser *Suffolk* managed to surprise the German raider *Karlsruhe* as she was loading supplies and guns onto the *Kronprinz Wilhelm*, a liner then in the process of being converted into an armed merchant cruiser. The two German ships immediately shot off in different directions. The *Suffolk*, rightly, followed the *Karlsruhe* – one of the fastest vessels afloat – but lost her in the haze.

The light cruiser *Birmingham* achieved a notable success on 9 August when she rammed and sank the *U15* approximately 100 miles off the Orkneys. *U15* holds the dubious honour of being the first U-boat sunk in the war.

The armed merchant cruiser the *Kaiser Wilhelm der Grosse* – previously the holder of the Blue Riband for the fastest crossing of the Atlantic – had slipped out of Bremen shortly after war began. Her time as an AMC was short as on 26 August she was caught by the cruiser *Highflyer* off the west coast of Africa. Despite being in a neutral harbour, the German ship was attacked and in just over an hour was reduced to a total shambles. Ninety of her crew managed to swim ashore before she turned over and sank.

The day after the destruction of the *Kaiser Wilhelm der Grosse*, the first units of the Royal Naval Air Service arrived in Ostend. Initially detailed to defend the British coast against Zeppelin attacks, the men of the RNAS were always more interested in offensive action and when, in due course, Ostend fell to the advancing German army, Commander Charles Samson and his men simply moved to Dunkirk, from where they waged war on the ground – in armoured cars – and in the air.

The first significant naval battle of the war took place on 28 August, when Admiral David Beatty took his battlecruisers – the *Lion*, *Queen Mary*, *Princess Royal*, *Invincible* and *New Zealand* – and an array of smaller support craft across the North Sea into the Heligoland Bight. Despite the shallow waters, the Battle of Heligoland Bight was a resounding success for the Royal Navy and for Beatty in particular.

The British plan worked perfectly. The light cruiser force from Harwich tempted the Germans to come out, expecting an easy victory, and then Beatty pounced. Three German cruisers – the *Ariadne*, *Mainz* and *Köln* – were sunk along with a destroyer. Several other German vessels were badly damaged and, in total, Beatty took 1,000 prisoners. His own losses were just thirty-five killed.

The German battlecruiser *Goeben*, which, a few days after war was declared, along with the light cruiser *Breslau*, ran the blockade of British ships in the Mediterranean and managed to reach Istanbul. It was a brave and risky enterprise, the skill of the German Admiral matched only by the ineptitude of the British commanders. A secret treaty between Turkey and Germany meant that the *Goeben* and *Breslau* were welcomed in Turkey which, as a supposed neutral country, should have immediately interned the two warships.

Opposite page: On the day that war was declared, Sir John Jellicoe was appointed commander-in-chief of the Grand Fleet. It was a crucial appointment. When reviewing the Battle of Jutland, Winston Churchill, First Lord of the Admiralty, later declared that Jellicoe was the only man who could have lost the war in a single afternoon.

THE PLUCKY LITTLE "GLOUCESTER" TACKLING THE "GOEBEN & BRESLAU" SINGLE-HANDED.

Despite the supposed 'heroic' actions of the cruiser *Gloucester*, as shown in the rather romantic postcard view above, no shots were fired during the chase of the *Goeben* and *Breslau* although the *Gloucester* was the ship that located the enemy at the western end of the Mediterranean and so began the long chase. The whole affair was one of misjudgment and muddle on the part of the British commanders. Integrated into the Turkish Navy, the threat of the *Goeben* as a force in the eastern Mediterranean remained for many months but, arguably, her greatest value lay in the embarrassment she had already caused to the British.

The cruiser *Amphion* along with the destroyers *Lance* and *Landrail* achieved the first British success of the conflict when, on 5 August they intercepted the *Königin Luise* as she was laying mines in the North Sea. Prior to the war, the *Königin Luise* had operated as a ferry out of Hamburg. *Lance* fired the first shots – the first British naval shots of the war – before the *Amphion*, a ship that had recently won the Fleet Gunnery prize, finished off the German minelayer. The cruiser then had to get between the terrier-like destroyers and the passenger vessel *Petersberg* that soon arrived on the scene, ferrying the German ambassador back home and therefore awarded with diplomatic immunity.

Early the following morning the *Amphion* joined the *Königin Luise* at the bottom of the North Sea. While her crew was still at breakfast, she ploughed head first onto one of the mines the German ship had laid the previous day. The surviving crew got across to nearby destroyers – including in their number Midshipman Fogarty Fegen, who was to win a posthumous Victoria Cross on the *Jervis Bay* in the Second World War – before the *Amphion* hit a second mine and sank. She was the first British naval loss of the war.

A rather romanticised German view of the *Königin Luise* and *Amphion* going to the bottom at the same moment. It did not happen that way but that did not stop members of the German public buying the postcard view in their thousands.

Opposite page: Mines had long been used in naval warfare but there had never been such extensive mining as now took place in the North Sea, at the eastern mouth of the English Channel and around the German coast. Mines were laid in clusters, fields as they were known, secured to the bottom of the sea or sewn indiscriminately and left to float in sea lanes where they might be expected to cause the most significant damage.

This contemporary print shows an RNAS armoured car raid into: German-held territory on the Western Front. This was the type of activity that suited Charles Samson down to the ground: hit-and-run raids that kept the enemy guessing – nobody knew where Samson and his men would turn up next.

Opposite above: The sad remains of the German armed merchant cruiser *Kaiser Wilhelm der Grosse* lie off the Spanish territory of Rio de Oro on the African coast. A luxurious and famous liner that had once held the Blue Riband, she had been converted for use as an AMC but her fine teak finish and high, spacious cabins were of little use in time of war. Surprised and battered to a pulp by the cruiser *Highflyer*, the unequal battle lasted under an hour and the German crew was lucky enough to be able to swim ashore to safety.

Opposite below: The Royal Naval Air Service was active from the early days of the conflict, taking the war to the Germans by air and by land. Instrumental in this aggressive policy was Commander Charles Samson, a man who had already made his name as a naval flier and who later went on to perform heroically in the skies over Gallipoli. By the end of August 1914, Samson was organising bombing raids on strategic targets and leading armoured car raids into German territory.

On 28 August, Beatty, in the *Lion*, led his battlecruiser squadron across the North Sea to surprise a German force in the shallow waters around the enemy coast. At the Battle of Heligoland Bight three German cruisers were sunk while the British sustained no casualties. It was the type of action that Beatty loved: a fast and hard-hitting raid that enabled him to show his flair and his ability to conduct 'hit and run' operations.

Opposite page: Admiral David Beatty, the flamboyant and charismatic leader of the British battlecruiser fleet. Not always the most tactful of men and certainly not someone who thought too deeply about the safety of his sailors, as far as the public was concerned Beatty was the epitome of the dashing naval officer. And, as might be expected in a man with such a gift for publicity, it was he who scored the first notable British naval success of the war.

HMS *Princess Royal*, one of five battlecruisers deployed by Beatty at: Heligoland Bight. It was the type of action for which she and her consorts had been designed: a battle where her speed and superior weaponry were decisive factors.

British sailors watch the end of the German cruiser *Mainz*, sunk during the Battle of Heligoland Bight. The *Mainz* has lost two of her funnels in the action and is clearly on fire. Not long after this photograph was taken, she heeled over and sank, joining her compatriots *Ariadne* and *Köln* on the seabed.

Some of the crew of the British Armed Merchant Cruiser *Laconia*, a former Cunard liner. They are obviously dressed for a fancy dress party.

Above: A close-up view of the battleship *Iron Duke*, flagship of Admiral Jellicoe. The size of the ship's massive 13.5-inch main armament can be clearly seen; these were weapons capable of throwing shells many miles through the air.

Opposite above: A congratulatory postcard commemorating the victory of the HMS *Highflyer* over the AMC *Kaiser Wilhelm der Grosse*.

Opposite below: The battleship *Erin*. Originally built for Chile as the *Almirante Latorre*, she was taken over by the Admiralty and renamed once war threatened in 1914.

H.M.S. TIGER

A 15 INCH SHELL FOR "LIZZIE'S" BIG'UNS (weight ONE TON)

Shells being taken on board ship.

Opposite above: HMS *Suffolk*, one of the ships hunting for the raider *Karlsruhe* in the Caribbean. When she encountered her one day, the German cruiser easily outpaced her before any damage could be done. The *Suffolk*, a County Class Armoured Cruiser, was typical of the outdated British cruisers, which were far behind the German ships in terms of speed and power.

Opposite below: The battlecruiser *Tiger*, along with the *Lion*, the cornerstone of Admiral Beatty's Battle Cruiser Squadron. In the eyes the of the British public she epitomised the speed and power of the Royal Navy.

A torpedo is launched. Both surface ships and submarines fired torpedoes, making them (along with mines) one of the most deadly weapons of the war.

Opposite above: Torpedoes, perhaps the most lethal weapon of the war, are shown here being manoeuvred along rail tracks towards the waiting ship.

Opposite below: Torpedoes are loaded on to a British submarine.

Sailors alter the direction of torpedo tubes on the deck of a destroyer.

Not all torpedoes were successful, and far more were fired than ever hit their target. This photograph shows a spent torpedo, dangerous now only if a ship should run into it.

September

September began badly for the Royal Navy. On the 3rd of the month, the torpedo gunboat *Speedy* struck a mine and sank off the Humber estuary while two days later, on 5 September, the cruiser *Pathfinder* was torpedoed by *U21* twelve miles south of May Island. It was the first German submarine success – against a warship – of the war.

The Royal Navy achieved some revenge when on 13 September Lt Cmdr Max Horton in the *E9* sank the German cruiser *Hela* off Heligoland. This was the first British submarine success of the conflict and Horton returned to his base at Harwich flying the Jolly Roger. Thereafter, displaying the pirate flag became the traditional sign of a successful submarine patrol.

If the month of September had begun badly for British naval forces, its final days were even worse and Horton's success was one of the few bright spots. On 19 September, Captain Max von Looff of the cruiser *Königsberg*, then lying secretly in the Rufiji Delta on the eastern coast of Africa, decided on offensive action. He slipped downstream and at dawn on the 20th, eased past the guard ship into the harbour at Zanzibar, where the old cruiser *Pegasus* was undergoing repair.

Before anyone knew what was happening the *Königsberg* had poured half a dozen salvos into the British ship. The *Pegasus* managed only a few shots in reply before, mortally wounded and blazing from stem to stern, she heeled over in the mud and sank. Job done. Captain Looff and the *Königsberg* quickly returned to their hideout in the Rufiji.

Just two days later, on 22 September, the *U9* torpedoed and sank three British cruisers in the shallow coastal waters off the Maas Lightship, all within an hour of each other. The *Aboukir*, *Hogue* and *Cressy* were old, slow and vulnerable to attack by submarines, but their sinking owed as much to the inability of their captains to appreciate modern warfare as it did to the design of the three ships.

Stopping to pick up survivors was clearly in the best interests of humanity and, after the first torpedo struck the *Aboukir*, it was exactly what the *Hogue* and *Cressy* proceeded to do. Unfortunately, it also made them perfect targets for the *U9*. In total 1,459 men were lost, a casualty list higher than that sustained on all ships during the Battle of Trafalgar.

In the Indian Ocean, the cruiser *Emden* had already begun her career as a raider, dozens of cargo ships having fallen to her guns. On 22 September the *Emden*'s commander, Karl von Müller, achieved a propaganda coup when he bombarded the oil refinery at the Indian city and port of Madras. Thousands of pounds worth of damage was inflicted on the refinery and von Müller slipped away before the hunting HMS *Hampshire* arrived on the scene.

Opposite above: Submarines, British and German, were active from the beginning of the war. To begin with, in the early months of the conflict, international law was followed and unarmed merchant vessels were usually stopped and their crews taken off before they were shelled, torpedoed and sunk. Warships were a different matter and these were attacked without warning. In early September the Royal Navy lost the *Speedy* and the *Pathfinder* to German torpedoes while Max Horton soon replied by sinking the German cruiser *Hela*. Even at this early stage, the value of the submarine was clear to all, but no one yet suspected the extent to which they would be used in the final two years of the war.

Opposite below: In terms of the number of merchant ships she sank, the German cruiser *Königsberg* was, perhaps, not the most effective commerce raider of the war but her mere presence on the coast of East Africa was a threat that the Admiralty could not ignore. There was always the threat that she would emerge from her hiding place in the Rufiji Delta to make a swift and sudden attack on convoys and ships travelling independently.

HMS PEGASUS.

In fact, when she did emerge in September 1914, *Königsberg*'s target was not merchant vessels but a Royal Navy cruiser. Admiral King-Hall's three-cruiser squadron – *Hyacinth*, *Astraea* and *Pegasus* – constantly patrolled this part of the Indian Ocean. The three ships were old and out-dated, *Pegasus* having been launched in the final years of the nineteenth century, and no match for a modern light cruiser like the *Königsberg*. When he learned that the *Pegasus* had put into Zanzibar for repairs, Captain Looff of the *Königsberg* seized his chance. At dusk on 19 September, he cast off his moorings and headed downstream to the open sea.

Opposite page: Winston Churchill as First Lord of the Admiralty. Churchill had become First Lord in 1911 when he immediately began to implement a series of long-term reforms. These included the development of naval aviation – he even took flying lessons himself – and the switch from coal to oil propulsion for ships of the Royal Navy. Churchill's friendship with Admiral Jacky Fisher, begun when Fisher was First Sea Lord in 1907, remained strong and few people doubted that, sooner or later, they would make a powerful fighting duo.

engl. Kreuzer „Pegasus" wird von dem deutschen
Kreuzer „Königsberg" bei Sansibar zerstört.

„Emden"=10 Pfg.=Spende. Mitteldeutscher Verband Weimar

Die „Emden", englische Handelsdampfer vernichtend
Originalzeichnung von Professor W. Stöwer, Berlin

„Emden"

Du kühner Streiter, Schiff ohne Ruh',
Ruhmvolle, tapfere „Emden" du!
Fährst auf dem Ozean rastlos umher,
Hast weder Hafen noch Heimat mehr.
Du bist unrettbar dem Tode geweiht,
Und wirst doch leben in Ewigkeit!

Lorbeer am Maste, Kreuze am Bug,
Zierde des Ozeans, der dich trug!
Springender Panther du, greifender Leu,
Urbild der Flotte ohn' Todesscheu!
Erz und Granit wird dein Bild übersteh'n
Nie wird dein Name verloren geh'n.

Wenn dich die Mehrzahl schmachvoll umkreist
Zeigtest der Welt du treudeutschen Geist.
Wie sie – die Deutschen – zum Sterben bereit
Dich, kraft des Mutes, vom Schrecken befreit
Wie aus dem Leben, die singend verweh'n
Blüten und Kränze des Ruhmes ersteh'n.

Wir, die erstaunend das Wunder ersah'n,
Fühlen durch dich unsre Rettung nah'n.
Herrscher der Meere, wo ist deine Kraft?
Wo deine Flotte, die „Emden" schafft?
Wir aber haben der „Emden" mehr –
All unsere Schiffe – die ganze Wehr!

J. Bermbach, Weim

Captain von Müller of the *Emden* soon grew tired of destroying merchant ships and decided on more warlike action. In the pre-dawn darkness of 20 September he carefully navigated his ship through the shallow waters off the Indian port of Madras. No one challenged him and when she was within range the *Emden* opened fire on the oil tanks of the port. Several hits were scored and millions of gallons of oil were destroyed before Müller decided he had done enough and once more slipped away out of sight.

Opposite above: At dawn on 20 September the *Königsberg* slipped into Zanzibar harbour and opened fire on the sleeping *Pegasus*. Salvo after salvo smashed into the British ship before anyone knew what was happening. Soon the ancient *Pegasus* was a blazing wreck. The *Königsberg* had turned around and sailed back out to sea before anyone could begin to organise an effective response to the attack. Captain Looff took her back to the sanctuary of the Rufiji Delta, where her reputation and her threat were greater than ever.

Opposite below: The most renowned and successful of the German commerce raiders was the *Emden*. Nominally part of Admiral von Spee's East Asiatic Squadron, the *Emden* operated as a lone hunter, ranging far and wide across the Indian and Pacific Oceans. In a four month career she sank nearly thirty merchantmen as well as a number of Russian and French warships and her name became a byword for adventure, romance and courage. The mere rumour of her presence in an area was enough to halt troop convoys and the British, eager to eliminate this threat, were forced to deploy dozens of vessels to hunt her down.

The loss of the three old armoured cruisers *Aboukir*, *Hogue* and *Cressy*, all torpedoed by the same U-boat on the same day, 24 September, caused yet more embarrassment for the Royal Navy. More importantly, the sinking clearly displayed the fact that this was a new type of combat against a ruthless and deadly opponent who could and would attack unseen and without warning. The *Aboukir* was sunk first, the other two, stopping to pick up survivors, quickly followed. This contemporary print shows the *Aboukir*'s Captain standing heroically on the upturned hull of his sinking ship. The British press was clearly trying to garner some merit from the disaster.

Opposite page: *Aboukir*, *Hogue* and *Cressy* were launched at the beginning of the twentieth century and were virtually obsolete when war broke out. They were products of their time, typical of the Admiralty's lack of forethought and dearth of interest in cruiser design. Nevertheless, their sinking brought howls of protest in the British press and cost the Royal Navy nearly 1,500 casualties. Among them was Lieutenant Henry Rennick, who had been a member of Captain Scott's last expedition in 1912 when he had shared a cabin on the *Terra Nova* with Birdie Bowers.

BATTLE-SHIPS LEAVING SCAPA, ORKNEY. 1909. T.K.

The ship's cat and some of the crew of the *Carmania*, an Armed Merchant Cruiser that was pressed into service at the start of the war. She fought the German AMC *Cap Trafalgar* in September and sank her.

Opposite above: The Armed Merchant Cruiser *Carmania*, which sank the German *Cap Trafalgar* in a ship-to-ship engagement on 14 September 1914.

Opposite below: Scapa Flow was the home of the British fleet at the start of the war.

Mines were one of the most deadly weapons of the war, both sides using them at will. This shows German sailors working with a mine – deadly and dangerous work.

Opposite above: The cruiser *Aboukir*, torpedoed with her two sister ships by the same U-boat, on the same day, within the space of one hour.

Opposite below: The monitors *Humber*, *Severn* and *Mersey*, flat-bottomed, shallow-draught vessels that were used to bombard land targets. Ugly and wallowing in anything like a heavy sea, the monitors carried out useful service with the Dover Patrol and in actions like the forthcoming Gallipoli campaign.

H.M.S. "ABOUKIR"

The King visits HMS *Barham* in the early days of the war. Royal visits were seen as good for morale but, with the Navy's natural insistence on 'spit and polish', they always meant extra work for the sailors. The royal family , with their German background, were keen to demonstrate their affinity with Britain's fighting forces.

Opposite above: Royal Marines landing in France. Marines were often used to augment soldiers, a policy that stemmed from the Crimean War in the middle of the nineteenth century, when their excellent showing endeared them to the public and to those in positions of power.

Opposite below: Leisure was very important, even in wartime. A steam pinnace from the cruiser *Hampshire* takes leave men ashore for a night on the town.

RINGING JACK ASHORE. STEAM PINNACE H.M.S. HAMPSHIRE.

E. HOPKINS.
SOUTHSE

Most of those who joined the forces enlisted in the Army but the Navy also needed men. This shows new recruits at Crystal Palace.

The recruits keep coming!

Get your head down when you can! An informal shot of sailors resting. It might be a posed photograph but the message was important. Look, also, at the scrawled and misspelt writing at the top left – a sorry reminder that war was not fun but a deadly serious business.

Torpedoes are inserted into the tube, ready for firing.

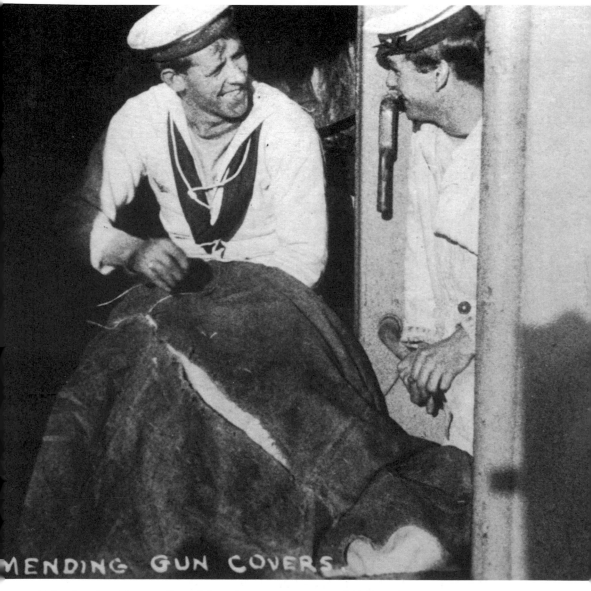

MENDING GUN COVERS

Being handy with a needle and thread was an important skill for sailors, perhaps as crucial as being able to load and fire a gun, read a compass or run up a signal.

Opposite above: RND recruits marching through London on their way to barracks. All the pomp and ceremony of the Navy.

Opposite below: 'No more coal dust,' says the caption to this photograph. Coaling was hated by all sailors, but the switch from coal to oil on many Royal Navy ships eased the despised task for most.

October

On 3 October the first units of the Royal Naval Division were landed to assist the Belgian Army in the defence of Antwerp. Included in the force was the poet Sub-Lieutenant Rupert Brooke of the Hood Battalion, his commission having been sanctioned by no less a person than Churchill himself. The fall of Antwerp, however, was inevitable and the Navy Brigade was soon evacuated, Brooke among them.

An RNAS raid, using Sopwith Tabloid aircraft, on the Zeppelin sheds at Düsseldorf took place on 8 October. Planned by Charles Samson and carried out by Flight Lieutenant Reginald Marix, two twenty-pound bombs were dropped onto the roof of the hangar, which burst into flames, totally destroying the partially built Zeppelin inside. Marix, his plane hit in twenty places, managed to get to within a few miles of his base before crashing. He then borrowed a bicycle and rode home.

On 15 October, the old and out-dated cruiser *Hawke* was sunk – another victim of the *U9* – while lying in a sheltered anchorage off the eastern coast of Scotland. There were many casualties on board the unsuspecting ship but seventy-five officers and men did manage to escape from the sinking cruiser.

An early destroyer action, foreshadowing later combats by the Dover Patrol, took place 40 miles to the west of Texel on 17 October. The light cruiser *Undaunted* along with the destroyers *Lance*, *Lennox*, *Legion* and *Loyal* encountered a German force and immediately closed for action. In a short but brutal encounter the German destroyers *T115*, *T117*, *T118* and *T119* were all sunk.

Just a day later the first bombardment of the enemy coast began when the monitors *Mersey*, *Humber* and *Severn* – shallow-draught vessels being built for Brazil but commandeered by the Admiralty when war broke out – started to shell the Belgian port of Ostend. Accompanied by other ships such as the destroyers *Nubian* and *Mohawk*, the three monitors continued the bombardment until 21 October.

On 18 October the submarine *E9* was destroyed by a U-boat and so became the first British submarine to be lost in the war. With the German underwater campaign beginning to gather momentum, on the 20th of the month, the steamer *Glitra* was the first British merchant vessel to be sunk by a U-boat when she was torpedoed by *U17*. Worse disaster was to follow.

On 27 October, the modern dreadnought battleship *Audacious*, completed only the year before, struck a mine while on gunnery exercises off the north-west coast of Ireland. As if to prove that they had learned from the recent torpedoing of the three cruisers, the rest of the squadron, including the *King George V* and *Ajax*, immediately left the area as, at that stage it was unclear whether the *Audacious* had hit a mine or been torpedoed.

Several unsuccessful attempts were made to take *Audacious* in tow, and with light beginning to fail, most of the crew were taken off. Fifty volunteers remained behind but by 6.30 in the evening with her quarterdeck awash and the ship rolling heavily, the rest of the crew were forced to leave. At 11.00 that night the battleship turned turtle and blew up.

The Admiralty, alarmed at the recent spate of naval disasters, tried to keep the news of the sinking out of the press and they maintained her name in the Navy List until the end of the war. Meanwhile, the crew were quickly distributed throughout the fleet and told to keep their mouths shut while the papers were informed that the *Audacious* had only been damaged.

It was no use as the liner *Olympic*, en route to Liverpool, witnessed the disaster – she was, in fact, one of the vessels that attempted to get a tow line across to the stricken warship – and the passengers, many of them American, could not be kept silent. Before long, the news of her sinking was the worst kept secret of the war.

Prince Louis of Battenberg, a man with many German connections, resigned as First Sea Lord on 28 October. He had been vilified by the British press for his supposedly pro-German views and finally decided that enough was enough. His replacement, who came into office two days later, was the seventy-one-year-old Jacky Fisher. It was a popular appointment, at least with the public, who were happy to see Battenberg go. As Fisher commented, Battenberg had only three friends – and two of them were Churchill and himself!

A man of great energy and strong opinions, Fisher had already served as First Sea Lord. He was vain and pompous and was by turns vitriolic and enthusiastic, but he was the man for the job and immediately set about galvanising the Admiralty.

The day after he took office, on 31 October the *Königsberg* was located hiding in the Rufiji Delta. Fisher marked it down for further action but at the very beginning of his tenure in office Jacky Fisher found out that he had other, more pressing concerns to deal with.

At the beginning of October, units of the Royal Marines landed to assist the Belgians in the defence of Antwerp. Churchill wanted to resign from the Admiralty and take up command of the new Royal Naval Division, a move that despite being supported by Lord Kitchener was quickly vetoed by the Cabinet. They were probably right. Within a few days it was clear that Antwerp could not hold and the Marines were evacuated.

Opposite page: After the fall of Antwerp, the trench system stretched for nearly 500 miles across Europe, and with most of Belgium now occupied, the tactical effect of bombardment from the sea was obvious. Three shallow-draught monitors, the *Mersey*, *Humber* and *Severn*, accompanied by smaller vessels, arrived off Ostend on the 17th of the month and began bombarding German positions. The bombardment lasted for four days although the effect of the shells on German positions was minimal.

BRITISH MONITORS IN
ACTION OFF THE BELGIAN
COAST.

Commander C. H. Fox had been the unlucky captain when the *Amphion* was sunk just twenty-four hours after war was declared. Transferred to the light cruiser *Undaunted*, he was again in action on 17 October, when his flotilla encountered four German destroyers. Fox immediately went into action – 'Am pursuing them,' was his message to the fleet. In a combat lasting barely ninety minutes the superior marksmanship of the *Undaunted* and her destroyers sank all the enemy ships. Fox's laconic message to his base read simply: 'Sunk the lot.'

Opposite above: With the increased use of mines it soon became clear that the risk to shipping was huge. As a result, dozens of trawlers and shallow draught paddle steamers, more used to carrying day trippers to and from parts of the coast, were requisitioned as mine sweepers. Many of these small vessels were lost during the next four years but they did an amazing job in clearing the sea lanes, an unheralded but very heroic part of the war effort.

Opposite below: Sweeping for mines was a time consuming and dangerous occupation, usually involving a sharp lookout and destruction of the mines by rifle fire. This view shows the crew of a paddle minesweeper attempting to deal with a mine by hand. Not until later in the war did more sophisticated techniques come into use.

As if to show that no ship was immune to the threat of modern weapons such as mines and torpedoes, on 27 October the modern dreadnought battleship *Audacious* struck a mine while engaged in exercises off the coast of Ireland. Despite the efforts of the crew, a volunteer party who stayed on board and the men on accompanying vessels which tried to take her in tow, it soon became clear that *Audacious* was doomed. All the remaining sailors were taken off and not long before midnight, *Audacious* turned onto her side and blew up.

Opposite above: Having endured enough disaster for one year, the Admiralty attempted to keep quiet the news of the sinking of *Audacious*. It was a hopeless task as the disaster had been witnessed by sailors and the passengers on the nearby liner *Olympic* and the news quickly got out. Despite this the Admiralty kept her in the Navy List right to the end of the war.

Opposite below: The hammocks of naval recruits, hundreds of them, in the halls of Crystal Palace. Hardly the best place to get a quiet night's sleep.

Germany's Battle Cry is

"*Germany over All*"

And her Navy drinks to

"*The Day*"

When she hopes to
Smash Britain's Fleet.

BRITAIN is FIGHTING

Not Only for the

FREEDOM OF EUROPE
BUT TO DEFEND
YOUR MOTHERS,
WIVES & SISTERS

FROM THE HORRORS OF WAR.

We must crush this idea
Of "GERMANY OVER ALL".

A Navy recruitment poster (Library of Congress). Hardly the most effective of posters, the first half concentrates on Germany's war aims and rather defeats the object.

Recruitment poster for the Royal Marines (Library of Congress). This would undoubtedly have appealed to the imagination of many men in 1914.

A recruitment poster for the Navy. (Library of Congress)

ROYAL NAVAL DIVISION

HANDYMEN TO FIGHT ON LAND & SEA

1ST BRIGADE	2ND BRIGADE
BATTALIONS:	**BATTALIONS:**
"BENBOW"	"HOWE"
"COLLINGWOOD"	"HOOD"
"HAWKE"	"ANSON"
"DRAKE"	"NELSON"
RECRUITS WANTED	**RECRUITS WANTED**

VACANCIES FOR RECRUITS BETWEEN THE AGES OF 18 AND 38

CHEST MEASUREMENT, 34 in.   HEIGHT, 5 ft. 3½ in.

PAYMENT FROM 1/3 PER DAY. FAMILY ALLOWANCES.

Besides serving in the above Battalions and for the Transport and Engineer Sections attached,

MEN WANTED

who are suitable for training as Wireless Operators, Signalmen, and other Service with the Fleet.

Apply to the Recruiting Office, 112, STRAND, LONDON, W.C.

EYRE & SPOTTISWOODE, Ltd., His Majesty's Printers, LONDON.

This Royal Naval Division recruitment poster details the eight RND Battalions, all of them named after famous admirals from the past.

There doesn't seem to be much 'play' evident in this recruitment poster for the RND (Library of Congress). Work, on the other hand, is what the RND is about.

A German painting from the early part of the war.

Opposite page: A German U-boat on patrol along the English coast. Despite the conditions, the submarine captain clearly prefers to remain on the surface.

The *Kaiser Barbarossa*, a German postcard. She is shown here a full speed and the amount of smoke from her stacks gives a good indication of what shell spotters would have had to cope with during a battle.

A Royal Naval destroyer at sea, seen here in a German postcard.

Torpedo boats were tiny craft that endured terrible conditions in the North Sea. Their crews were usually wet and cold and their war went largely unrecorded and unheralded.

A German artist's impression of the sinking of a British merchant ship. In reality the U-boat would hardly have been likely to have been this close to her victim.

Opposite page: A British dreadnought.

The old battleship *Prussen*, shown here on a German postcard.

Opposite page: The destruction of a British merchant ship. Commerce raiding was vitally important to the German war effort and, after the surface raiders were hunted down by the Royal Navy, the destruction of merchantmen was left largely in the hands of the U-boats.

HMS *Warspite*, one of the massive Queen Elizabeth Class battleships. Launched just before the war, she went on to fight at Jutland and in the Second World War.

Opposite page: A torpedoed steamer, shown here in a German artist's painting.

This German painting from 1914 gives a good indication of the cold and wet endured by the U-boat crews. Perhaps more importantly, this painting was a harbinger of what was to come as the U-boat campaign gathered in intensity during the second half of the war.

RIFLE DRILL OF MARINES

Marines parade for rifle drill on the after deck of a battleship. There was always a need to keep the men active, particularly when the Grand Fleet were in port for such long periods.

Opposite page: On 31 October, Admiral Jacky Fisher returned to the Admiralty as First Sea Lord, a position he had previously occupied with much success until his retirement in 1910. Prince Louis of Battenberg had been the incumbent for several years but his pro-German outlook and lack of dynamic leadership meant that his time in the post was limited. Churchill knew that he wanted Fisher and he duly appointed him to the job two days after Battenberg resigned.

TABBIE IN THE GUN MUZZL

Ship's pets were common. Everything, from cats and dogs to birds and monkeys, was kept by sailors. The ship's pet on the German cruiser *Dresden* was a pig. It was appropriated by sailors from the *Glasgow* when *Dresden* was sunk and, because of its hairy coat, was given the nickname 'Tirpitz'. This photograph shows Tabbie, the ship's cat, in a gun barrel on the *Queen Elizabeth*.

Opposite above: Officers and men of the *Queen Elizabeth* gather together on and below the ship's 15-inch guns.

Opposite below: The most noticeable thing in this photograph is not the sailors or the massive guns of the *Queen Elizabeth*, but the ship's cat, which stalks imperiously along the gun barrel.

OFFICERS AND CREW of H.M.S. "Q.E."

THE CATS PROMENADE

November

The hunt for von Spee, commander of the powerful German East Asiatic Squadron, had been left in the hands of Admiral Christopher 'Kit' Craddock, who was based at the Falkland Islands in the South Atlantic. His force consisted of the light cruiser *Glasgow*, the armed merchant cruiser *Otranto* and two old armoured cruisers, the *Good Hope* and *Monmouth*, neither of which had the speed nor the weapons to take on von Spee's *Scharnhorst* and *Gneisenau*.

After repeated requests for reinforcement, Winston Churchill sent Craddock the old pre-dreadnought *Canopus*. She was, he said, a 'citadel' around which Craddock could base his fleet. In fact she was old, slow and manned almost exclusively by reservists who had never even fired her guns in anger.

Craddock sailed for the Pacific without the *Canopus* and, on 1 November, encountered von Spee off the Chilean town of Coronel. In a wild sea that made the lower gun ports of the *Good Hope* and *Monmouth* totally unworkable, the Battle of Coronel was a one-sided affair that lasted barely an hour. Both the *Good Hope* and *Monmouth* were blown out of the water and went down with all hands. None of the five German ships suffered damage of any sort. It was the first British naval defeat for over a hundred years and created a furore both in the national press and in the Admiralty.

On 3 November, two naval bombardments took place, although they were many miles apart. Firstly, an Anglo-French force including the battlecruisers *Indefatigable* and *Indomitable* along with the French *Suffren* and *Verite* undertook a prolonged bombardment of the outer forts at the Dardanelles. Churchill had already laid plans to attack what he regarded as the 'soft underbelly' of the Central Powers forces at Gallipoli but this early bombardment – which was neither followed up, nor of any real strategic importance – served only to warn the Turks what was coming.

The second bombardment was by German battlecruisers which made a swift sortie across the North Sea to shell the Norfolk coast. It was the first attack on the British mainland and one British destroyer was sunk when it hit a mine while attempting to intercept the German force as it returned to its base.

On 7 November the besieging Japanese forces (helped by the British battleship *Triumph*) at last took the German-held port of Tsingtau on the coast of China. Tsingtau was Germany's only toe-hold in the area and was, nominally at least, the base of von Spee's Squadron. The siege had lasted for several months, virtually since Japan joined the conflict on the side of the Allies in August 1914, and confirmed von Spee in his decision that, if he wanted to survive, he would have to adopt a roving commission in the South Seas.

On 9 November the cruise of the *Emden* finally came to an end when she was caught and sunk by the Australian cruiser *Sydney*. The raider was attempting to destroy the cable and wireless station on the Cocos Islands in the Indian Ocean and her landing party was still ashore when the *Sydney* came into view.

The *Emden* had operated as a lone raider for three months, destroying nearly thirty merchant ships, sinking several Russian and French men-of-war and terrorising the Australian and New Zealand governments into cancelling vital troop convoys. Her captain, von Müller, had always known that his time was limited but in those few short months he had intrigued the world and run the British forces ragged.

The day after the destruction of the *Emden*, plans to destroy the other raider *Königsberg* were finally put into place. The old collier *Newbridge* was escorted into position and sunk across the main channel of the Rufiji Delta, thus blocking the *Königsberg*'s route to the sea. From then on she would be something of a sitting duck, marooned several miles inland – provided the British could get the right ships to bombard and sink her.

Accident also caused losses at this time. On 26 November the pre-dreadnought battleship *Bulwark*, lying at anchor in Sheerness, was suddenly ripped apart by an explosion and sank almost before anyone knew it. She had been taking on ammunition and the explosion was probably caused by the overheating of cordite charges that had been stacked adjacent to a boiler room bulkhead. Out of a crew of 758 there were only twelve survivors.

Admiral von Spee's squadron is shown here moored off the Chilean port of Valparaiso just before the outbreak of war. The Germans would return to Valparaiso after the Battle of Coronel.

Opposite above: Admiral Christopher Craddock had been hunting in the Pacific for the German East Asiatic Squadron for several months. He knew that his squadron was desperately out-gunned by von Spee's fleet, in particular by the modern cruisers *Scharnhorst* and *Gneisenau*, and continually asked the Admiralty for reinforcements. He expected the modern armoured cruiser *Defence* – he got the old, out-dated pre-dreadnought *Canopus*. So when Craddock and von Spee finally came to blows off the Chilean port of Coronel on 1 November, *Canopus* was miles behind and Craddock sailed into battle with little hope of victory.

Opposite below: Christopher 'Kit' Craddock was a Yorkshireman whose avowed wish was that, when his time came, he would die in action or on the hunting field. A romantic yet also a realist, he buried his private papers in the garden of the Governor of the Falkland Islands before setting off around the Horn to meet von Spee.

Admiral von Spee
Kommandant des Geschwaders im großen Ozean

The Battle of Coronel lasted barely an hour. With the British ships outlined against a setting sun and in a wild sea that made their lower gun ports virtually unusable, Craddock's two armoured cruisers, the *Good Hope* and *Monmouth*, were blown apart by superior German gunnery and lost with all hands. Only the light cruiser *Glasgow* and the armed merchant cruiser *Otranto* escaped in what was the first British defeat in a major ship to ship action for over a hundred years.

Opposite page: Admiral Maximilian von Spee was an astute and capable commander who knew that, whatever success he might achieve, the glory would be short-lived. If he beat Craddock he was sure that the British would hunt him down and, far from home and without dockyard repair services, the end result for him and his fleet was bound to be disastrous. Such thoughts would never prevent him from doing his duty and when, late in the afternoon of 1 November, he saw the smoke of Craddock's ship, he knew they had a battle to fight.

Suwo (flag)   *Tango*   *Triumph*

Suwo (flag)   *Tango*   *Triumph*

Bombardment of Tsingtau
(*Drawn by W. Bevan*)

For the first three months of the war, the raider *Emden* had led a charmed life, sinking merchantmen almost at will. Men like her Captain von Müller and First Lieutenant von Mücke had become household names right across the globe. The Admiralty might declare *Emden* and her crew to be pirates but even the British press, with their liking for the underdog, had a sneaking admiration for the isolated and lonely ship.

Opposite page: Two sketches by the marine artist W. L. Wyllie show the bombardment of Tsingtau. The German base at Tsingtau on the coast of China was, in theory at least, von Spee's home port. The German admiral, however, knew that with Japan joining the war on the side of Britain, the port would quickly become a bottleneck and so opted for a wandering commission in the Pacific. Tsingtau was besieged by Japanese forces and bombarded from the sea. After a siege of several months, the port and its fortress surrendered on 7 November.

THIERICHENS.

V. MÜCKE.

V. MÜLLER.

MEYER-WALDECK.

V. SPEE.

WEDDIGEN.

Die Helden
unserer Marine

Verlag von
Gustav Liersch & Co.

The *Emden*'s luck finally ran out on 9 November. Arriving off the Cocos-Keeling Islands, Captain Müller sent von Mücke ashore with a landing party to destroy the British wireless station. And there the raider was surprised by the RNAS cruiser *Sydney*. In a short and brutal action, the *Emden* was battered to defeat and the hulk left to rot away on the reef. Von Mücke and his landing party took control of an old sailing ship and, after many adventures, managed to make it back home to Germany. Von Müller went into captivity for the rest of the war.

Opposite page: A composite German postcard showing, among others, Captain von Müller, Lieutenant von Mücke and Admiral von Spee. Such was the success of the German ships in the southern seas during the first few months of the war that men like these became heroes in their native land.

HMS *Dreadnought*, the most revolutionary of battleships when she was launched in 1906 but already obsolete when war began in 1914. Nevertheless she did manage to sink the *U29*, whose captain had previously torpedoed the *Aboukir*, *Hogue* and *Cressy*.

Opposite above: The battered remains of the *Emden* lay on the reef off Keeling Island for many years. In shark-infested waters there was little attempt at salvage and she lay there, slowly rotting and rusting away, until well after the Second World War.

Opposite below: The success in ending the career of the *Emden* was offset a few weeks later when, on the 26th of the month, the battleship *Bulwark* blew up while at anchor in Sheerness. There was a terrible loss of life in what was an accident rather than enemy action. Nearly 800 men went to their deaths because of the careless packing of cordite charges on board the anchored ship.

The White Funnel paddler *Glen Avon*, taken into service with the Navy as a minesweeper – a far cry from ferrying day trippers around and across the Bristol Channel. Dozens of paddle steamers and trawlers were used by the Admiralty during the war and many were sunk.

Opposite page: Looking out over the quarter deck of the cruiser *Hampshire*, one of the ships engaged in the hunt for the *Emden*. Marines and sailors have assembled for a ceremonial event. Even in wartime the Navy adhered to its traditions.

Quarter Deck and Crew of H.M.S. "Hampshire"

H.M.S. BULWARK

The raider *Karlsruhe* was regarded as one of the fastest ships in the world and, despite being hunted by many British vessels, she was never caught. Towards the end of 1914 she blew up, mysteriously, while on her way to bombard the British-held island of Barbados – yet another example of the dangers of badly stored ammunition.

Opposite above: The battleship *Bulwark*, destroyed by an internal explosion in November 1914. The disaster killed hundreds of sailors, and showed the dangers of careless storage of ammunition.

Opposite below: HMS *Hogue*, a photograph taken before her destruction in the first year of the war.

Oakley, Photo, Copyright,   Troops at Sonthampton.   Netley, Southampt

Der Kreuzer
„Scharnhorst."

A Royal Naval Air Service balloon or blimp on patrol over the Channel. As the war went on, the use of aircraft and balloons by the Navy increased dramatically. They were the ideal way to locate lurking submarines and then either drop bombs on them or call in destroyers to attack the enemy. Patrols over the North Sea, Atlantic and even the English Channel were long, arduous and boring – unless, of course, the balloon crew happened to spot a U-boat.

Opposite above: Troopship at Southampton. As the war went on, more and more soldiers were sent to France. Most of them went on hastily requisitioned troopships, but the Navy, usually with destroyers and trawlers, had to protect them during the crossing.

Opposite below: The *Scharnhorst* at speed, a classic view showing the raw power of the German ship.

LOWERING 15 INCH SHELLS INTO MAGAZINE – Q.

The job of any battleship was to destroy enemy warships. Therefore, the guns and ammunition were the most vital elements of the vessel. This photograph shows sailors lowering 15-inch shells into the magazine of the *Queen Elizabeth*.

Opposite above: On the deck of a partially completed capital ship, workmen stand and watch or go about their tasks.

Opposite below: Tying knots or splicing; sailors always had jobs to do.

A submarine submerging. Most submarines, British and German alike, spent as much time as possible on the surface. Because of short battery life, their time below the waves was limited. Conditions in the cramped hulls were appalling, and the submarines were much slower when submerged than when travelling on the surface.

Opposite above: Officers and crew on the conning tower of submarine B5. The boat is about to dive and the men are making ready to descend into the cramped hull of the submarine.

Opposite below: The B5 submerging, with the after part of the submarine already below water.

M107.3   JUST BEFORE DESCENDING INTO HATCHWAY.

M107.4   MAKING READY TO SUBMERGE.

OFFICER AT EYEPIECE OF SUBMERGED SUB

Once submerged, a submarine was blind – until it was able to raise its periscope. This shows an officer staring through his 'eyepiece', surveying the surface. Raising the periscope could be dangerous, as observant watchers could spot the protruding device or the wake caused by water rushing past it.

Opposite above: The B5 arrives back at its base after a patrol. In the early part of the war most submarines had short range, and cruises were, of necessity, of short duration.

Opposite below: The 15-inch guns of a giant British battleship are trained on the enemy.

SUBMARINE ARRIVING AT SUPPLY BASE. M107

M10A-12   15 INCH NAVAL GUNS

December

On 8 December, the Royal Navy meted out revenge for Coronel. It was an example of Churchill and Jacky Fisher at their best. With amazing speed and enterprise, the battlecruisers *Invincible* and *Inflexible* were detached from the Grand Fleet and sent south to rendezvous with a hastily assembled squadron of armoured cruisers. Under the command of Admiral Frederick Doveton Sturdee, previously chief of staff at the Admiralty, the battlecruisers were heading south less than a fortnight after the news of the disaster at Coronel reached London.

The fleet arrived in Port Stanley in the Falkland Islands on 7 December. Early the following morning, while the British vessels were still re-coaling, the masts of Admiral von Spee's cruisers were spotted offshore. The *Canopus*, now beached on a mud bank as a guard ship, opened fire, the German fleet fled and Sturdee ordered a general chase.

During the course of a long and arduous day von Spee's ships – the *Scharnhorst*, *Gneisenau*, *Nürnberg* and *Leipzig* – were hunted down and sunk. Von Spee went down with his ship (along with his two sons) and only the light cruiser *Dresden* managed to escape.

On 13 December Lt Norman Holbrook, commanding the submarine *B11*, threaded his way through the Turkish minefields at the entrance to the Dardanelles. When he torpedoed and sank the Turkish merchantman *Messoudieh* he was awarded the Victoria Cross. It was the first VC of the war given to a submariner.

The German High Seas Fleet was not yet totally confined to its base and on 15 December a large force of battlecruisers and heavy cruisers, under the command of Admiral Hipper, left port and headed across the North Sea. Using a thick sea mist for cover, they made landfall on the north-east coast of England and proceeded to sail down the coast, shelling at will.

Scarborough, Hartlepool and Whitby were all bombarded; thousands of pounds worth of damage was caused and 120 people were killed. Hipper, well contented with his day's work, then made off across the North Sea. Attempts to intercept the German force proved ineffective and they duly made harbour undamaged.

On Christmas Day 1914, while the infantry on both sides were enjoying their unofficial truce in No Man's Land, nine seaplanes of the RNAS mounted a bombing raid on the Cuxhaven naval base. The aircraft had been transported to the German coast by seaplane tenders, the aircraft being lowered into the sea for take-off. The raid was not particularly successful, most of the bombs falling well wide of the target, but the exercise did at least force the German Navy to disperse its fleet along the full length of the Kiel Canal.

British revenge for defeat at the Battle of Coronel came on 8 December. Acting with his usual alacrity and imperiousness – and with the full approval of Churchill – Jacky Fisher detached two battlecruisers, the *Inflexible* and *Invincible*, from the Grand Fleet and sent them southwards under the command of Admiral Frederick Doveton Sturdee. Strict radio silence was observed and when, on the 7th, the capital ships and their attendant cruisers arrived at Port Stanley in the Falkland Islands, von Spee had no idea they were there. The very next day, von Spee decided to attack the Falklands and was amazed to see the tripod masts of the two battlecruisers in the harbour.

Frederick Doveton Sturdee had been Chief of Staff to Prince Louis of Battenberg and, along with his chief and Churchill, has to bear some of the blame for failing to send adequate reinforcements to Kit Craddock. There is, however, no truth in the rumour that Jacky Fisher – who, admittedly, did not like Sturdee – said 'Sturdee caused the mess, let him go and sort it out!'

The German flagship *Scharnhorst*, a vessel that, along with her sister ship *Gneisenau*, was more than capable of dealing with out-of-date armoured cruisers like the *Good Hope* and *Monmouth*. Against the fast, well-armed and protected battlecruisers that the Royal Navy now deployed against them, it was a very different matter.

Having seen the enemy capital ships and realised what their presence meant, von Spee fled southwards with Sturdee and the whole of his command chasing them for all they were worth. The 'Long Chase', as it was called, took hours and several of the British ships came near to running out of coal. But gradually, one by one, the German cruisers were overhauled and destroyed. *Scharnhorst, Gneisenau, Nürnberg* and *Leipzig* were all sunk, only the speedy light cruiser *Dresden* managing to escape over the horizon.

Opposite: Admiral von Spee, on the *Scharnhorst*, went down with his ship. His two sons, Otto and Heinrich, young officers just starting on their careers and serving on the *Gneisenau* and *Nürnberg*, also perished in the Battle of the Falkland Islands. About 2,000 German officers and men were drowned or were blown to bits along with them.

Die beiden Söhne des Admirals Graf von Spee
Leutnant Graf Otto von Spee   und   Leutnant Graf Heinrich von Spee
an Bord S. M. S. „Nürnberg"   an Bord S. M. S. „Gneisenau"
starben den Heldentod in der Seeschlacht bei den Falklands-Inseln
am 8. Dezember 1914.

F. Urbahns,
Hofphot.
Kiel

Despite the British 'distant blockade' of Germany, it was still possible for German ships to evade the watchers. On 15 December, a large force of German battlecruisers under Admiral Hipper sortied out across the North Sea. In a thick mist, they closed on the British coast and opened fire. With British forces hampered by the mist, Hipper was able to sail down the coast and shell Scarborough, Hartlepool and Whitby before heading back to his base. As this composite view shows, damage was inflicted on many houses as well as the lighthouse and castle at Scarborough. While over 100 civilians were killed, the real damage was to the morale of the British public. Mainland Britain, so long sacrosanct, was suddenly vulnerable to attack – nobody, it seemed, was safe.

As 1914 drew to a close, Winston Churchill, from his desk at the Admiralty, could look back on five months of war with decidedly mixed emotions. There had been successes but there had also been dismal failures, and Churchill knew that the months and years ahead were not going to be easy.

Christmas 1914, not a truce perhaps, but still time for sailors to relax.

"BOTTLED UP!!!"

Trying to make light of a humiliating experience, a British postcard laughs at the battlecruiser *Goeben* which, after avoiding the British ships in the Mediterranean, was now apparently 'bottled up' in Istanbul.

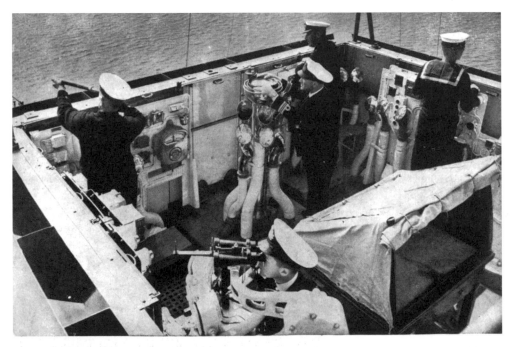

The navigation bridge of the battleship *Royal Oak*. She might be a modern battleship but like the smaller cruisers and destroyers of both British and German navies, officers and men invariably worked in the open air.

Above: The cruiser *Donegal*, complete with dazzle paint – a view from later in the war.

Right: On 21 November 1914, three British airmen from the RNAS – Briggs, Babington and Sippe – attacked the giant Zeppelin sheds at Friedrichshafen, causing considerable damage.

The Canadian Pacific *Montezuma* disguised as HMS *Iron Duke*.

Opposite above: Part of the German fleet, dressed overall. The ship in the foreground is the cruiser *Dresden* that fought at the battles of Coronel and the Falkland Islands.

Opposite below: German prisoners on the dockside in France. Transporting enemy prisoners across the Channel quickly became another task for the Royal Navy.

93 GUERRE DE 1914. — *Officiers Allemands prisonniers*

Reproductioninterdite

LL.

Die Abrüstung der Deutschen Flotte.
Munitions-Abgabe.

Phot. W. Feyerabend.
Wilhelmshaven

Gymnastics on a gun barrel – nerves of steel needed for this piece of tomfoolery.

Opposite above: German ships loading munition at Wilhelmshaven. Loading ammunition and coal were back-breaking tasks for the sailors of all navies.

Opposite below: A squadron of German torpedo boats lies moored and waiting for the call to arms.

The battlecruiser *Invincible*, one of the two capital ships sent by Jackie Fisher to take revenge on the fleet of Admiral von Spee.

Opposite above: The destroyer *Oak*, just one of the many small vessels in the Dover Patrol. As the war went on, the Dover Patrol increasingly became a vital part of British coastal defences.

Opposite below: Ferrying wounded soldiers back to 'Blighty' was an essential service carried out by the Royal Navy. This shows a hospital ship at night.

The launch of the battlecruiser *Queen Mary* on the River Tyne, September 1913. Ships continued to be launched throughout the war, adding to the fleet and providing moments of celebration for those living in dockyard towns.

Opposite: A view of HMS *Dreadnought.*

THE BRITISH NAVY'S PIGEON POST

A British Submarine Officer sending a message by a carrier-pigeon

A British submarine, the *D1*, with the crew standing on top of her.

Opposite: Pigeon post! A carrier pigeon is released by the crew of a British submarine. In the days before radio, it was often the only way to get messages back to base.

A photograph of the HMS *Iron Duke*.

Opposite: Sir George Callaghan, who was replaeed by Lord Jellicoe. He was considered to be too old for the role.

A group of sailors on board HMS *Ajax*.

Opposite above: The German battlecruiser *Von der Tann*.

Opposite below: A German gunboat.

Three men in a barrel! Even in wartime, sailors could still have fun – and, of course, the rum ration was still in place throughout the war.

Opposite above: Another RNAS bombing raid took place on Christmas Day 1914, when nine seaplanes attacked the German Naval Base at Cuxhaven.

Opposite below: The Grand Fleet at sea; it was a powerful and much feared fighting force.

A training exercise – get fit at all costs – in Crystal Palace football stadium.

Opposite: A First World War sailor postcard, bought in its hundreds by lonely matelots – and by their partners back home in Blighty.

On 8 October 1914, Douglas Spencer Grey led a raid on Cologne, flying almost 200 miles into Germany to destroy part of the railway station. This artist's impression shows Grey high above the famous Cologne Cathedral.

HMS *Queen Elizabeth* slides into the water. For the dockyard maties, it's a case of a job well done, now on to the next one.

The mountings for guns can be clearly seen in this detailed photograph, taken during the building of HMS *Queen Elizabeth*.

Opposite above: Admiral von Spee fought a brave combat against superior forces at the Battle of the Falkland Islands. The result was inevitable defeat for the German squadron. This painting shows the end of the *Scharnhorst*. Von Spee went down with his ship.

Opposite below: The end of the cruiser *Leipzig* at the Battle of the Falkland Islands.

Shipbuilding during the war years. Producing new ships was an essential task, but, as casualty lists grew, dockyard maties often came in for criticism from the public and the press. At Pembroke Dock in Wales, for example, the local paper called the dockyard a 'funk hole' and declared that the men who worked there would do a better job fighting in the trenches.

Sailors assemble for inspection on the deck of the battleship *Queen Elizabeth*. Routine and tradition were important, the cornerstones of discipline, and were regarded as the things that would see the 'British Tar' through all manner of tight situations.

GUN DECK OF H.M.S. Q.E. M106-18

As well as their main weapons, battleships like the *Queen Elizabeth* were equipped with secondary armament in order to defend against torpedo boat attack. This shows the 6-inch gun deck of the *Queen Elizabeth*, low to the water and a wet, cold station for any sailor.

Opposite above: Hoisting shells from a lighter into the *Queen Elizabeth*.

Opposite below: Cordite charges being hoisted on board. Notoriously unstable, cordite caused many explosions on board ship when it was hastily or carelessly stowed.

The guns of the *Queen Elizabeth*, the first British warship to mount a massive 15-inch armament. It made her and her sister ships the most powerful battleships in the world.

Sailors take a moment's rest on the 6-inch gun deck of *Queen Elizabeth*.